I AM A WEALTHY WOMAN
BECAUSE
I REFUSE TO BE ABUSED

I AM A WEALTHY WOMAN BECAUSE I REFUSE TO BE ABUSED

MY ROAD TO ACHIEVING TOTAL PROSPERITY

By: Jean Marlo Davis

XULON PRESS ELITE

Xulon Press Elite
2301 Lucien Way #415
Maitland, FL 32751
407.339.4217
www.xulonpress.com

Unless otherwise indicated, Scripture quotations taken from the King
James Version (KJV)–*public domain.*

Paperback ISBN-13: 978-1-6628-2649-8
Ebook ISBN-13: 978-1-6628-2650-4

DEDICATION

I WANT TO DEDICATE this book to my precious mother, Minnie Gamble, who recently got her wings and is on her next assignment. I did it, Mom. It took years, and as I promised you, I did it. And I know I would hear you say, "Well done, Jeannie."

I want to say thank you to my husband, Bruce Davis, for always believing in me and telling me I am the bomb, and I can do anything! Because of you, I found my voice again and I begin to believe again. I am so grateful to God for your love and support. I love you, honey bunches, now and forever.

Thank you to my Financial Father's Alvin Curry & Ivey Stokes who truly taught me about finances, investing and creating wealth. You brothers are the giants who shoulders I stand on. Thank you!

I thank God for my four beautiful children, Jada, Darryl, Vincent, and Darnell. You four have always been the wind beneath my wings. Everything I have done in my life has been for you guys. Mommy loves you very much, and I am so grateful to God for my four beautiful babies.

To my unborn grandbabies and my current grandbabies, Selena, and Sofia, I am so glad you guys will never know poverty, lack, fear, or doubt because we teach you that you can Have, Be, and Do Anything. Nana loves you and will always work to make sure every generational curse is broken, and we have "indestructible wealth" for generations to come.

I want to thank the Management and Staff at Chateau Elan Winery in Braselton, Ga. For all your support and taking exceptionally good care of me when I would work on my book at the Chateau, and I would fall asleep exhausted by the fireplace. You guys looked out for me and encourage me In a way that most establishment wouldn't. It's the going the extra mile for me. That's why Chateau Elan is a second home for me. Thanks Guys!

To my fans, thank you for believing in me, supporting me, purchasing this book, and always sharing your testimonies with me. It is because of you I do what I do. One billion lives impacted. It is done!

TABLE OF CONTENTS

INTRODUCTION

F OR BETTER OR worse, for richer or poorer, 'til death do us part…well, that is what marriage is supposed to be. Unfortunately, you never think that you are going to get divorced years later and find yourself in financial ruin. Yet, after a divorce, many women find themselves living below the poverty level.

You may ask, "Why?" Well, we are so loving, caring, and trusting that we never learn what the family business is all about. We trust our husbands to take care of us, 'til death do we part, but little do we know that some men have property in several states, offshore accounts, and money stashed away for a rainy day. Sometimes you won't see a dime of that money or will be begging in the courts for alimony to be able to take care of you and your three or four children that you have as a result of the marriage. You may find yourself helpless because you don't know a lot about money, investments, or being business savvy.

Let's back up for a second and let me tell you the situation I was in years ago that has inspired me today to be a "Wealthy Woman."

When I was eighteen years old, I met a man during my senior year of high school, and I thought I was going to spend my whole life with him. He was kind and generous, and he always made me feel like a woman, regardless of my age. I was young and naive, and I pretty much believed everything this man said because he was a doer—he didn't just talk it; he walked it too. I was excited because he was older than me and he was a person I could look up to.

After a couple of years of being with him, I really trusted him, and we fell in love and got married. Now, we went through some good times as well as bad times, however, this man, let's say Chris (name used to protect identity), was very determined when it came to making money. Chris was good with his hands, and he could build or fix anything without limitations. Years passed by, and after hard work and dedication, Chris landed the contract he had always dreamed of. The contract he received paid him a generous amount of money, and he became so busy that he had to hire ten people to work for him. Eventually, he developed his own construction company. He would hang sheet rock, lay tile, do floors, paint, fix buildings, etc. Chris was the

big man with the money, and he was well respected…
just know he developed a huge ego as well.

As far as myself, I went to college for business management, and I worked several government jobs. One
of those jobs was working as an IRS agent, where I
had the responsibility of examining and auditing tax-
payers. I was determined to start my own business
one day; I just needed to be placed on the right track.
Mainly, I supported Chris with his business. I helped
him with payroll and taxes, and I worked full time as an
assistant manager for a small apartment community. I
was young and very determine to win!

One day, the worst thing you could ever imagined
happened to Chris. The equipment he used for his
company was stolen from storage. The police stated
that it was an inside job, since the locks and bolts had
not been tampered with, so perhaps someone who
worked at the storage company took his equipment.
A lack of equipment posed a huge problem for Chris
because he worked for the apartment community
and the apartments needed to be punched, painted,
and repaired. The office manager at the time was very
patient, and she expressed to Chris that she was sorry
and told him to let her know what he would do by
Wednesday.

I could get into all the particulars of that situation, but I won't waste your time; I need to get to the point. Wednesday came, and the manager was getting a little eager because we had residents who were ready to move in that weekend. She talked to Chris to see what his plans were, but she was dissatisfied with his answer. Listen to this, now—this is the killer: that Friday, because nothing had been resolved between Chris and the manager, one of Chris's own employees went to the manager and offered to do the job that needed to be completed. Chris lost the contract, and his pride and dignity went with it. The question now was, how was Chris to explain this to his employees, some of whom had wives who were pregnant? What would he say or do to justify his ego trip and his failure to negotiate a deal that would be a win-win situation for the manager and himself? Chris couldn't take it. He was angry as hell, and because we lived on the property of the apartments for free, we were asked to move out or begin paying rent immediately.

Well, you could give that up, Chris was not going to pay rent or stay there, so we had to move. What did I do? I had to support my husband. Sadly, Chris and I were already having problems in our marriage. I knew he wouldn't support me still working for the manager who fired him, so I quit my job and went along with his plan.

Later, Chris found a home for us, but it was a fixer upper and was going to take weeks to get it ready for us to move in. Chris contacted one of his friends and asked him if we could move in with him until the house was ready, and the guy agreed. We moved in.

During this time, Chris was truly angry and bitter. We were arguing every day, there were no resolutions in sight. At this point, I just didn't know what to say or do to just give his mind some peace. I was scared—we had four children in the picture, and the picture was looking grim with no peace in sight.

Chris was receiving phone calls from his employees about what was going on with the job. They wanted to know when they would start work again, and it was just a big mess. I was petrified! I was so helpless because Chris was barely working on the fixer upper that we were going to move in because we had to leave the property where we were staying because we were no longer employees. Chris and I was arguing every day. I was living in fear of what would happen next.

LIFE-CHANGING EVENT

Never would I ever have imagined that this would happen to me and my four children! One day, Chris told me he was going to wash clothes. Most of our things were in storage, so at his friend's house, we had very little with us. While Chris was putting things in the van, I noticed that my wallet with all my personal business, ID, and credit cards was gone. I looked around the house, and I realized that my shoes were missing, the children's shoes were missing, and our clothes were gone too. I ran downstairs to see what was going on, and Chris jumped in the van and pulled off. At that time, pagers were the means of getting in touch with someone, rather than a phone, so I just started paging and paging Chris. He had a voicemail service, so I left several messages on his voicemail. In a panic, I ran to his friend and told him what had happened, unable to breathe and scared as hell. The friend told me to calm down, saying that maybe Chris just left to clear his mind and would be back shortly.

I knew, I knew Chris was not coming back; otherwise, why would he have taken my things? Why would he have left me at his friend's house? For the life of me, I just didn't understand what was going on...I was lost. My children were there with me; two were sleeping, and two were playing outside. The two who were playing outside had their shoes on, but Chris had taken the shoes of the two who were sleeping. All we had were the clothes on our back—no money, no job, and no place to live.

What the hell was I to do? I asked myself, "How in the hell did I allow myself to get in this mess?" I had no time for tears, no time for fear. It was either do or die. I had four children who depended on me and had nothing to do with this terrible situation. For a moment, I was confused, thinking I would lose my mind. I felt weak and helpless. I wanted to fight someone, I wanted to hunt down Chris and beat him for leaving us. How dare he punk out and leave me with these precious babies? How dare he?!

Chris had always promised me that he would never leave me or our children. I kept hearing a voice in my head saying, "Don't cry, get your ass up, and take care of those babies." Although I was so scared, amazingly, no tears would form. I couldn't get one tear to drop. Even though I tried to cry, it wouldn't happen. I felt like a robot that had been given a command and couldn't stop until the objective was complete.

It was only my four babies and myself. I remember getting up the next morning and walking downtown to DFACS (Department of Family and Children Services). I spoke to a representative there, explaining the situation, and she assigned a caseworker to me right away. My pride was killing me—I didn't want to be there! I believed in work first, not welfare. I didn't want to get any food stamps or a "welfare check." The caseworker came out and took me to her office. She gathered all the facts, then came up with what she could do to assist my children and me. She signed me up for food stamps and told me I would get a check to help me get on my feet. I told her I didn't need the check, that I was perfectly able to get a job—hell, I was educated, with plenty of work and business experience. I just needed a little time. However, she didn't hear a thing I said; she simply stated, "Ma'am, you qualify for this assistance. Take it and think about your children, not your pride!" I shut up…

I didn't want it, but I needed it. That low-down man had left me, and I was a ship without direction. My caseworker told me I would receive food stamps in a couple of days and emergency help, then they would help me find a job, if I had any problems doing so on my own.

Step one was completed—the children had food coming and money as well. Now I needed to proceed to step two—time to find a place to stay. I contacted my good friend Sharon and told her about the situation. She came to my rescue. I will always love her dearly for that! Sharon told me she would allow my four children and me to stay with her until I got on my feet. She was angry as hell with Chris too and probably would have hunted him down and caused him serious damage. She told me that she would pick us up after work the next day and take us to her house. Oh Lord, I was so thankful to my God, my Father. God answers prayers! Step two was completed…

JOURNEY BEGINS

That night, it began to rain really badly, raining cats and dogs, as the elders would say. I was sitting in front of a big picture window, and the children were sleep. The house was very peaceful, and a sense of calmness came over me. Out of nowhere, I heard a loud, piercing noise. I had never heard such a sound before. Tears begin to flow heavily, and soon I was on my knees. The noise had come from me! Chris's friend ran out of the bedroom. I think he was in his under-wear, and his girlfriend came out too. All I know is he grabbed me and begin to rock me like a baby. He consoled me and told me everything was going to be alright. I guess that sound came from all the built-up pain and anger that had been inside me. Once I had gained complete security for my children, I was finally able to exhale and breathe again. In my heart, I knew that everything would be alright. I was in good hands, and those were God's hands. I knew I had nothing to fear because God would never leave me.

The next day, my friend Sharon came and picked up my babies and me to take us to her safe and secure home. She was a single mom with four children of her own, but she never said she didn't have room for us. She allowed me to stay there until I could get on my feet and get my own place. She gave me a fighting chance to start all over again. Sharon was my "guardian angel."

I will always love and respect her. She did more for me than some family members would have done! By God's grace, I was given a "fresh start."

This began my journey into realization—realizing why it is important to have financial intelligence, financial literacy, and financial savvy. I thank God for that terrible mark in my life. This trial helped shape me into a powerful woman, a woman with grace and confidence, a woman who believed in herself, a woman who knew she would achieve what she willed, a Wealthy Woman.

I want the reader to understand that you too must become a wealthy woman, a wealthy person! You must understand how to create generational wealth. This book is to teach you practical principles to help you achieve financial freedom. I pray that you implement the knowledge that I have been blessed with and through my pain, your healing can begin. This is not a book of misery, male bashing, fear, or doubt. This is a book to help you achieve total prosperity in every area of your life! Not just financially, but mentally, spiritually, emotionally, and physically. You must have the complete prosperity pie; one slice is not enough! You have to have wisdom, knowledge, and understanding in this world. Ignorance is not forgiven or allowed. The information in this book will help you achieve victory over your past, present, and future endeavors. You are now being placed on the path that will help you become a Wealthy Woman! Why? Because you refuse to be abused!

Chapter 1

REALIZATION

"What doesn't kill us makes us stronger!"

HOW MANY TIMES have you heard that state-ment? You usually don't think about that quote when you are going through a trial or an obstacle, but after every trial, there is a great lesson and growth.

The lesson I learned is that I must do something to empower my children and myself. I realized that "if it is to be, it's up to me!"

I want you to reflect on those words: "if it is to be, it's up to me." You must realize that regardless of whether you are married, single, with or without children, or whatever your situation is, <u>you</u> are the biggest factor, which means if it is to be, it is up to YOU. For change to come, you must make a change in your situation. Don't pity yourself or feel like all hope is lost. Get up, have no fear, and realize that all things are possible. All you need to have is faith, belief, and, of course, knowledge.

THE AWFUL TRUTH!

I want you to know the truth and begin to change your life today! This is the "awful truth," as I have researched it over the years and found these alarming statistics…

According to the Per Ellevest article "What Women Can Do about Divorce Inequality," Women's finances dip 41 percent after divorce. The Pew Research Center says that in 69 percent of heterosexual marriages, husbands make more money than their wives. If a couple divorces, the woman's total household income drops more than the men.

The Forbes article titled "The 6 Nasty Financial Surprises for Divorcing Women" states that 46 percent of divorced women surveyed by Online Marketplace Worthy said that divorce brought them financial surprises. 1,785 adult women were surveyed. 22 percent of the women were 55 or older, and most of those had already been divorced.

The six nasty surprises divorcing, and divorced women often encounter are:

1. Being unaware of the total size of their marital debt, including the primary mortgage, credit cards, debt, 401k, loans, student loans, etc.
2. Not anticipating they would have to return to the workforce.
3. Assuming child support and/or alimony would be higher or last longer.
4. Assuming they could keep the marital home.
5. The staggering cost of health care insurance.
6. Underestimating the cost of getting a divorce.

SO, WHAT DOES ALL THIS MEAN?

Statistics show us that we totally depend on our spouses, partners, family members, our jobs, or the government for financial security. We struggle like hell to take care of our husbands and children, yet we end up killing ourselves from dissatisfaction and are not at ease, which equals disease. There are many single- family households in America, as well as an alarming increase of obesity in women. We are carrying our own weight and the weight of our families, while literally killing ourselves from a lack of wisdom, knowledge, and understanding concerning finances and health—mental, spiritual, and physical.

It is time to wake up and realize that we must begin to take better care of ourselves and begin to start doing something for ourselves!

After researching and finding these statistics, I was so angry that I just couldn't wait until my book was out to share this knowledge with others. I began to take immediate, massive action by starting my Wealthy Women Conference. I had my first meeting January 31st, 2009, in Smyrna, Georgia. I was so excited to share this information with women of all walks of life.

It was a small, intimate setting; however, the information that was shared was powerful. I started with the women a Course of Action Plan, issued financial statements, went over the difference between assets and liabilities, and then discussed the cashflow quadrant that Robert Kiyosaki teaches. We covered so much that day, and the inspiration shared by Latonya Muhammad was absolutely astounding. Let me tell you, it was information, inspiration, and a Course of Action. I then decided to have these meetings every month. Women are in need of understanding and increasing their financial IQ. We need to surround ourselves with successful businessmen and women so we can begin to take our lives to the next level. I plan on touring all over the world to educate the mothers of civilization. You know the saying: "When you teach a man, you teach just that man; however, when you teach a woman, you teach a nation!"

I realized that through constant teaching and studying, no nation can rise higher than its women!

It is time to understand that in life, we must have total prosperity in every area of our lives; again, that's mentally, spiritually, physically, financially, and emotionally.

BIG WAKE-UP CALL

A good friend of mine named Kim told me that she depended on her husband to take care of all the responsibilities of their household. He paid the mortgage, utilities, car notes, and insurance; started savings accounts for the children and investment accounts; etc. What could she say? The man was an excellent provider. She could use the money she made from her job for herself and the children. She told me that she never paid bills at all; rather, she just spent her money on the family. She was so blessed to have a man who loved her and her children so much. She was very thankful for this awesome provider.

She never imagined that her worst fears would come true. Her husband suddenly died of a heart attack, leaving her with all the responsibilities of the house. Oh, she told me she thought she was going to lose her mind. What was she to do? She had never handled the finances of her household. Now, this beautiful lady had to plan a funeral and bury her husband; take care of two mortgages, car notes, and utilities; and deal with investors, estate planning, 401k's, and IRAs. She felt like she had a heart attack and died also!

My friend Kim told me all she wanted to do was run into a hole and never come out again. Now, you think this might have been the worst of her concerns, but imagine family members fighting over property and money, plus explaining to your children that daddy's not coming home anymore. I know that God was with Kimme because that is the only way she could have made it through that terrible time.

As I stated earlier, what doesn't kill us makes us stronger. There was definitely a lesson to learn in all of this for Kim. She realized that she needed to increase her knowledge about money and finances so she would never end up in this situation again. This hardship put her on the road to becoming a Wealthy Woman.

I want you to know that I pray nothing like this ever happens to you; however, please do not allow yourself to be like a chicken waiting to be plucked. Robert Kiyosaki, a well-known multimillionaire, and financial educator, teaches that when you have no financial intelligence, that is what you become—a chicken. When you don't have knowledge, anyone can sell you any financial product, investment, or deal, and you are unable to grade the investment to see if it will yield you the rate of return you are looking for.

When my ex left me busted, disgusted, wrecked, and in a mess, I decided that I would begin to empower myself with knowledge that I could use to take care of my babies and myself. Most women would be angry and bitter at this man for the rest of their lives, yet I refused to allow "my past to put my future in a wheelchair." I am thankful to God for all the experiences He has given me, but make no mistake; although educational, it was very, very painful as well. Still, the pain gave birth to a powerful reality. I am traveling all over the world educating men, women, and children on how to lower taxes, get out of debt and create generational wealth. My goal is to empower women to become wealthy. I have worked with Actor/Activist Mr. Danny Glover, Ex Minnesota Vikings Football & Businessman Fran Tarkenton, and Multi-millionaires Ken Rolfness, and Jack Zufelt, and so many others (these are powerful men I have worked with).

Realize that the power to change your life is in you so you can help others change theirs. I am living proof of that. Nothing just happens!

Chapter 2

THE MORE YOU KNOW; THE FURTHER YOU GO!

I REMEMBER HEARING MY mentor speak to a live audience and he stated that degrees are subject specific and just because you are a doctor, lawyer, teacher, business owner, or other respected professional, that does not mean you know anything about finances. He went on to say that if you couldn't swim, do you think you could get a book, read it, and then be able to jump in the water and start swimming? The audience responded by saying no because we realized that in order to be successful, we must be taught, then trained.

I honestly believe in my heart that if a person knew better, they would do better. I believe that when it comes to finances, debt, wealth creation, or just life principles, a lot of our problems exist simply because of ignorance. When you are ignorant, that doesn't mean you are dumb; it just means that you are unlearned in that area. Financial education is the key to success. I would rather spend thousands of dollars on my financial education than waste money on clothing shoes, or, you know, "doodads" that will not yield me the return that I am looking for. It is time to examine the philosophy that says, "The more you know, the further you go."

Imagine having Donald Trump's knowledge, Robert Kiyosaki's knowledge, or Oprah Winfrey's knowledge...your life would change in an instant. When you acquire a certain type of knowledge, you change frequencies, just like a radio station. When you first get a channel on the radio, you must start off on a lower frequency, but when you begin to grow, audiences become greater, you receive more financial support, and you will fortunately need to switch channels to a better frequency to reach a higher level or group of people.

"WHAT'S YOUR FREQUENCY LEVEL?"

When I was single and struggling like hell, I was working a job I hated, only to get home and have to feed the children, give them baths, help them with homework, put them to bed, and prepare for the next day. It was a total nightmare. It was like that movie *Groundhog Day*–the same day played over and over and over with no relief in sight. I felt like a prisoner in my own life. I thought that if this is the way life is supposed to be, then let me out of this nightmare. Make no mistake, I love my children, and I was incredibly grateful for every minute of the day I was blessed to be with them. That love I have for my children is what made me desire a better lifestyle for them.

I remember having a family meeting with my children and asking them what kind of mother they thought I was. They all said nice things about me, but I told them to be honest and let me know what they honestly thought. All my children told me they loved me, that I was a great mom, a hardworking mom, and a loving mom; the only thing they said that they wanted from me was "more time." Understand that I worked a full-time job and a part-time job, as well as running a part-time business at that time. I was hardly home.

In my head, I felt I was providing for my children, giving them a nice, safe, clean environment, and I was the sole provider. I thought I was doing the right thing for my children, so to hear them tell me they needed "more time" was a shock to my system. I began to feel so bad and trapped because I didn't know what I needed to do. I prayed over my situation because I knew I had to change "frequencies." My channel was being forced to change. Therefore, I created a plan to leave my job in the next ninety days. Now, I wouldn't advise any of you to just quit your job, of course, especially if you are not willing to pay the full price to win! In my mind, I had no other choice. I left my job on August 23rd, 2003, with nothing more than the next paycheck coming, my plan, my vision, and my core desire to win. My four children motivated me and took the fear out of me. I changed frequencies. I started on the road to Financial freedom. Failure was not an option!

"Be Careful, Lock Those Wings.
Vultures Are Waiting!"

When I left my job, I was so excited. I told myself, "Self, you can't quit, and if you quit, you better not say a thing to anyone else about your dreams." Well, my mother didn't raise a quitter, but I will tell you, the fear was there—the fear that I would fail, and people would laugh at me and say, "I told you so." Then I had a thought: *The hell with that; I promised myself that I would fight like hell to win and I would keep God first, seek His guidance, and network my world.*

Free is power! The power of offering free service and doing things for free will open up a lot of doors for you. If you just give from the heart, doors you never imagined will open for you. I believed in my vision, I believed in my skills that I had acquired from life, I believed in myself, and all I needed was that big break where someone would give me a chance to shine.

That chance came with one of the most generous radio stations in Atlanta, Georgia. WRFG 89.3 FM gave me the opportunity to come on their show to share my knowledge about taxes, finances, and wealth creation to anyone who would listen to the sound of my voice. Brother Wanique Shabazz and Brother Ackon, just to name a few, would allow me to give the listeners tax and financial advice because of my years of training with financial institutions, being an ex-IRS agent, and being a business owner.

I was very grateful, and still am, to this station because a lot of my client base came from those listeners. I was brand new in business, and I wanted people to know who I was and what I had to offer. I tell you, it seemed like when one door opened, several trials were on the other side. Guys, you have to be serious in business! One of my pet peeves is when people say they are in business, yet when you ask for a card, they don't have one. You have to be locked and ready to roll because you are the representative of your business, nobody else. I had to make that point…now, back to the trials.

I was afraid, money was tight, clients were few, and failure was chasing me. I was running as hard as I could to catch success. I would sometimes think to myself, *Jean, have you lost your mind? You can always go back and get a good job!* I just knew in my heart that I wasn't going to give up and going back to a job would not do. I knew there was a bigger and better plan for me in life, and as my mentor told me, the only way for you to go out of business is to quit fighting. I knew that regardless of what happened in my life, I wasn't going to stop working toward my goals.

I remember a story about the eagle: when a storm comes, the eagle locks his wings and flies through the storm, making it safely to the other side. Well, you know that eagle feels a lot of turbulence, but I believe the eagle's mind is made up to succeed. See, my name is Jean Marlo Davis, and what that spells is Success! Many people don't want you to achieve your dreams and goals; they will tell you, "You are a fool for starting that business," "Just get a good job," or "Be realistic now, you know you can't do that." Listen to me now, if someone you know begins a sentence with what you can't do, then do me a favor and run! When you are giving birth to an idea, you don't need any negative energy around you, and you don't need to share your goals and aspirations with everyone either because not everyone is happy for you. Not everyone wants you to succeed!

Take my advice and lock your wings and fly through the storm. If you stay focused, you will make it to the other side, which is success. But remember, the vultures are always waiting for you to fail!

Chapter 3

THE SECRET TO YOUR SUCCESS IS IN "THE POWER OF NETWORKING"

I WISH SOMEONE WOULD have shared the concept of networking with me when I was much younger. If they did, I would have made my millions years ago. I have met so many powerful people by going to networking meetings. Networking is meeting other people who are striving to build businesses, have products or services to offer, or have skills that you can utilize. When you network, you really raise the bar on your personal development as well as your business skills. I urge everyone reading this book to attend networking events. Go to these events and meet as many people as you can, gather their cards, and give them your business information. Only begin to share your ideas, concepts, and what you have to offer after they have shared with you in great detail what they are looking for and you have developed a relationship with them. You will be very surprised who you meet and how you can connect with someone who can lead you to a connection that can empower you and your business.

I remember when I first started my business, TIFFIS, LLC (tax, finance, and wealth creation company), I was invited to a networking event with business owners from all walks of life. We were able to walk around the room and meet people and share with them what we had to offer to the marketplace. I was able to meet so many people who needed my help in their businesses that I went from zero clients to ten clients in one night. I was excited! I was even able to help other business owners who didn't need my services by giving them referrals of people who might need their services. I learned a powerful lesson that night: because I gave great service to those ten clients, they went on to refer many more clients to me, then this process became viral. One after another, people became aware of who I was and wanted my services.

My mentor taught me that people will do business with people they know, like, and trust. Your business will grow based on how you treat people in your "personal network."

Someone once asked me, "Jean, how do you advertise?"

I simply answered, "I don't; I use <u>word of mouth</u>!" I am giving you this principle because if you learn to utilize the power of networking, this will make you a wealthy woman.

DEVELOP A STRONG NETWORK

You want to develop a strong network, and this doesn't just relate to business; it relates to every area in your life. You need to meet people who are movers and shakers; people who are spiritually grounded; people who are intelligent and focused; people who are financially free; people who have a high self-esteem; people who are loving, caring, and understanding. You need to meet people!

Here is a perfect example: Oprah Winfrey has a huge network. If she wants to help her audience with physiological problems or emotional issues, she has Dr. Phil. For money problems, she brings Suze Orman. When in need of a decorator, she has it; for an accountant, she has it; for management, she's got that too! The list goes on and on. Look where she is now—a brilliant, savvy billionaire who adds value to the lives of thousands of people.

Oprah's huge network has made her a very wealthy lady because she understands the "science of business." You too can learn from this example. Oprah has expanded her mind, her spirit, her skills, her talents, and her God-given abilities. Please add as many people as you can to your network. Make sure they add value to you, and, in turn, you add value to them as well. This will help you grow as a person while also helping you with your personal development, which is another strong key to being successful. We will discuss personal development in the next chapter.

Here is a second example: A good friend of mine, Mr. Ken Rolfsness, who is a multimillionaire, asked me if I would like to participate in a 100-city tour he was putting together to help educate people about how to make money in network marketing. He knew I was an ex-IRS agent who taught people on the tax advantages of their home-based businesses. He said, "Jean, you have a very powerful service and product you can offer to the people." Well, you know I told Ken I would be extremely excited to be on the tour. He told me he was still working on the speakers and would let me know when he was ready. Long story short, a few months later, Ken called me. He said, "Jean, we are ready to start the tour. Here are the speakers who are going to be a part of the Show Me the Money Tour." Ken started reading the names. I couldn't believe that I would be going on tour with Mr. Danny Glover, Jack Zufelt, and the Powerful Ken Rolfsness! I was so ecstatic, I couldn't explain it to you, even if I tried.

Great partnerships are built through working relationships. Working with these powerful men has really had a great impact on my life. Jack Zufelt taught me so much about how to expand my vision, develop my way, and grow my business. Danny Glover just really shocked me; I've never met a more selfless, heart-giving man. He has become like a father to me. He really broke down the power of residual income. Ken Rolfsness…what can I say about him? If he believes in you, he is like a walking billboard for you; at least, that is what he is to me and so much more. I can't even dive into the depths of our relationship, what he has done for me and my family, the connections he has given to help me expand my business, and so much more. He is even married to a great woman! Ken, you are the best. These people have been very influential in my life and have opened doors that have been a total blessing to me. You couldn't put a price on these wonderful relationships we all have developed through the power of networking.

Remember, it is not always what you know, but who you know that makes all the difference in this world! Never, ever, ever, ever mistreat people you know. Don't burn bridges; always be the person willing to give the solution, as this makes a huge difference as well. Be careful how you treat people; everyone is important. You never know, the person you mistreated could be the person who could have expanded your personal network, cash flow, business, or even life!

Imagine you have a million-dollar idea or concept, and you don't know what to do with it yet. You haven't met the right people or agent who can help you. You decide to just get out and meet people and experience the networking life. You go to an event, you meet person after person, they share what they do, and you do as well. Next, you meet a person who shares with you what he does, and you discover this is the person you need to work with. You make a powerful connection that you feel in your gut will help you with your business venture. You have just discovered for yourself firsthand one of the many tools for creating wealth.

It would be so easy to write a book on the power of networking instead of just a chapter. If you don't remember everything about this chapter, just remember that the people you know are what shape your future. If you don't like where you are, you might need to change the people you are with! Make new friends, make new decisions, network, network, and when you get tired, network some more. If you ask any successful person how they became successful, they will probably tell you that they did a lot of networking to expand their network. You can become a remarkably successful person by embracing what I just shared with you about networking.

Don't be set in your ways. Explore your options and learn to "network your world."

Chapter 4

PERSONAL DEVELOPMENT: YOUR INCOME IS ATTACHED TO YOUR PERSONAL GROWTH

I T'S AMAZING TO me how people spend thousands of dollars on junk and doodads but refuse to invest in their own personal development. However, you, sitting in that chair, reading this book, congratulations! You have discovered another key to becoming wealthy. Remember how Mom and Dad used to say, "Reading is fundamental?" I often wonder, *What did they mean?* I am sure you have seen those commercials that say, "The more you know, the farther you go." These statements are so true. Reading is fundamental, and the more you know, the farther you will go. Not knowing can harm you and stop your growth. You have to start working on your personal development. When you work on yourself, you begin to grow, and your income will grow as well because you are adding value to the marketplace.

How do I do this, Jean?

Quite simply: begin by creating a library. Buy books that are inspirational and informational, books that will help you expand your knowledge base. There is so much you can learn by reading and taking notes as you read, then applying the knowledge you just learned. Your library shows exactly where you are in life and where you are going. Make sure you have a visual library with videos on demand, as well as an audio library with CDs or mp3's, and of course, your reading library with your books. I get so excited when I read books or listen to CDs that help me achieve my goals. To me, that can sometimes be better than having a consultant because you can always go back to your library and pull-out material for a subject you need to research without having to pay a consultant fee. The internet is another great source to gather information from as well, for everything you want to know about any subject is on the internet.

OPE

OPE stands for other people's experiences. This is a good way to help you develop your personal strengths. Have you ever heard phrase "youth is wasted on the young"? What do they mean by that? Well, I bet you have caught yourself saying, "If I knew when I was twenty what I know now, my life would be so different." Well, our experiences teach us what to do and what not to do to get ahead in life. Some of us are still experiencing the same trials because we have yet to learn the lesson from our experiences. To me, life is the sum total of our experiences. When you sit down and talk to elders, teachers, mentors, or family members and they share their experiences with you, you should take notes.

OPE help us in so many ways:

1) They save us time and energy because if we truly listen, we can gain knowledge from their experiences without having to go through them ourselves.

2) They save us money, especially if you are striving to make investments or deals that are similar to the person who has already done what you are striving to do. If that person is a good source, the tips they give you could save you thousands, even millions, of dollars.

3) The wisdom you gain from OPE is awesome. I have taken so many notes from going to workshops and seminars and talking to my mentors that when I am faced with a similar situation, I am able

to grab my resources, review them, and make the right decision.

4) They help you achieve your personal goals much faster, because you don't have to make the same mistakes. This cuts down on the time it takes to learn the lesson in the first place.

As I stated, you can learn so much from other people's experiences. Pay attention, listen more, observe more, take notes, and begin to apply the knowledge you just gained. Don't keep making the same mistakes; that's just foolish, especially if you have a road map directing you in the way you should go.

OTHER PEOPLE'S SUCCESSES & FAILURES (OPSF)

Wow, this is an awesome way to learn and to grow. I have read many books on people who are now where they want to be in life. Oprah Winfrey, P Diddy, Obama, Russell Simmons, Rev. Ron, family, mentors, teachers… the list goes on and on. I could spend the rest of this book writing down everyone I have tapped into for knowledge. Just reading about their struggles and what they did to succeed sends shock waves through my body. My mind begins to spin; ideas begin to flow! OPSF is the power of success, and when you read about other people who have found success, you should feel like if they can do it, then you can do it as well. If you learn from successful people and apply what you learn, you will be successful too!

How about other people's failures? Can you learn from people who fail? Absolutely! If you learn what exactly they did to fail at a certain project, goal, or aspiration, and really pay attention to their processes, you can avoid some of the mistakes they made. In school, we were taught that F's are bad and failure is unacceptable. No one told us that we should make as many mistakes as we can, so we learn not to repeat those mistakes. I tell my children all the time, "If you make a mistake, learn from it, or you are doomed to repeat it!" I know you have heard that insanity is continuing to do the same thing while expecting different results. You have to be willing to change. Don't beat yourself up for failing or making mistakes. I want you to make as many mistakes as possible; just promise me you will learn from them and move on to bigger and better things.

STOP HAVING PITY PARTIES!

Everyone has struggles, pains, and failures, but the people you read about who have experienced these obstacles are the ones who overcame all the obstacles they met along their path. After all, you are created in the image and likeness of God, and you have the power to make your life what you want it to be.

I want you to remember that the reason I encourage you to work on your personal development is because you are representing yourself. People are buying you, not your product or service! You are the gatekeeper to your own success. If you don't have the believability, the audacity, the confidence, or the "swagger" about yourself, who do you expect to attract? Be strong and believe in yourself; I believe in you. I believe you are stronger than you think you are. The world is waiting for you–remember that! New adventures, new discoveries, are at your feet.

Develop your skills, your talents, and your abilities, for personal development is a strong key to being a wealthy woman. Therefore, work on yourself day and night, and if there is something you don't like about yourself, change it. You have the power, so make it happen. No excuses. We are waiting to meet the new and improved you! Command your existence, demand your respect, observe your mistakes, and create your world. You are a Wealthy Woman–a force to be reckoned with!

Chapter 5

INCREASING YOUR FINANCIAL IQ: WHAT'S YOUR GRADE?

REMEMBER HEARING MY mom say, "A fool and his money will soon part." Later, I understood what she was saying: if you don't understand how money works and fail to increase your financial knowledge, you will be broke!

Have you ever wondered why many people who hit the lottery and win millions end up broke in just two years? I was told you have to first become a millionaire in the mind, because if you acquire the money before increasing your Financial IQ, you will lose it. Have you taken a look at your current finances and given yourself a report card? Would you even know what to look for or how to grade yourself?

In order to get your mind in the right place about your finances, here are some questions I want you to ask yourself:

- Do you have a financial statement?
- What does your financial statement look like?
- What are your liabilities?
- What are your assets? (Trust me, your house isn't one if you currently live there, unless you rent it out.)
- Do you totally depend on yourself for all of your income?
- How do you define wealth?
- How do you achieve wealth?
- If you lost your job today, how long could you live off of your assets?
- Lastly, are you building generational wealth?

Make sure you answer these questions truthfully because the truth will set you free. Answering these questions will help you create your report card, or shall I say, your financial statement.

I will begin to help you by answering these questions in an overly simplistic way so you can understand.

What is a financial statement?

A Financial Statement (financial report) is a formal record of the financial activities of a business, person, or other entity.

Relevant financial information is presented in a structured manner and in a form that is easy to understand. It typically includes basic financial statements.

1. Statement of financial position: also referred to as a balance sheet, reports on a company's assets, liabilities, and ownership equity at a given time.

2. Statement of comprehensive income: reports on a company income, expenses, and profits over a period of time.

Now, here is an example of a financial statement:

Income Statement

Lists sources of income, i.e., salary, interest, dividends: Real Estate, Businesses.

Expenses

Taxes
Mortgage
Student Loan Payment
Credit Cards

Car Note
Child Expenses
Bank Loans
Etc.

Balance Sheet

ASSETS	**LIABILITIES**
Savings	Home Mortgage
Stocks/Mutual Funds	School Loans
CD	Car Loans
Real Estate	Retail Debt
Business	Mortgage
Etc.	Bank Loans
	Etc.

I like how Mr. Robert Kiyosaki makes this diagram easy to understand; he uses the example of a report card.

INCOME	EXPENSES
ASSETS	LIABILITIES

As I stated before, if you live in your home, your home is a liability, but if you rent it out, it becomes an asset.

This comprehensive report allows you to truly see whether you own an asset or a huge liability. It also allows you to truly visualize where your money is going so you can begin to have your money working for you, rather than working for your money.

What are liabilities and assets? Simply put, liabilities constantly take money out of your pockets, while assets put money into your pockets.

Understanding what assets and liabilities are will help you to begin creating wealth.

What is wealth? Wealth is the collection of income-producing assets that allow you to live the type of lifestyle you desire, regardless of going to work.

Income-producing assets are an example of passive income, which is income you can depend on that does not require a lot of your time. This is income that allows you to do something one time and continue to get paid on it.

For example, income-producing assets could be acquired through investing in apartment complexes (real estate), investing in businesses (being a joint venture or angel investor), being an author or songwriter, investing in land, etc.

So, we see investing is big. Now, think about…

Network marketing!

Oh wow, most people don't like that word. Well, did you know that 80 percent of the members of Congress own a home-based business? Most network marketing or Multi-Level Marketing (MLM) are home-based businesses. Did you know people like Robert Kiyosaki back MLMs? Suze Orman, Warren Buffet, Greg Norman, and so many other wealthy millionaires and billionaires all participate in network marketing.

Network marketing is a business that allows you to partner with likeminded people who offer products and services to the masses. This allows you to pay a one-time investment and have low overhead. It always comes with a corporate structure you don't have to manage, which allows you to make residual money from repeat sales. Most MLMs are licensed to do business in US and Canada, as well as many other countries, and this enables you to open new points of distribution and distribute your product and/or service to the masses. What I love most about this investment, which I teach people all the time, is that it is a personal development company with a compensation plan attached to it. The personal development training you receive comes from people who have experienced what you are going through and who have achieved wealth in the business. They too will teach you how to succeed, and they have an invested interest in your success.

As an ex-IRS auditor, I will tell you that if you go into business with the intent of making a profit, and you materially participate in the operation of the business, you qualify for hundreds of tax deductions. This is a powerful business investment.

I asked you a question earlier, which I would ask again: if you lost your job today, how long could you live off your assets? If you tell me, "Not long," or if you don't have any assets, then it is time for you to start building right now. I would like to suggest network marketing, MLMs, or home-based businesses, because these are some of the most lucrative ways to build an excellent asset overtime. Eventually, with the right knowledge, skills, training, and personal development, you could create generational wealth. This structure allows you to still work your day job while also working on your fortune part-time. You will learn how to attract customers and business owners, build business in various states and countries, develop diversification, and grow personally.

Remember, your income is attached to your personal growth. We can no longer depend on social security, 401k's, and relatives to take care of us. You can start changing your financial future right now. You must work on increasing your Financial IQ. By doing so, you will begin to understand how money works, and you can now invest the money you are earning from your part-time business in other streams of income. The idea is to work your full-time job while also working part-time on your fortune, turning your home-based business into a cash cow!

If you are looking to partner in a home-based business and don't know which one, contact our office, and we will get you started with a powerful vehicle to help you create wealth. I not only believe in home-based business, but I also participate in one as well.

We are using the vehicle of network marketing to help thousands of people become financially free. Contact us to get started with this powerful vehicle with one of the fastest growing companies in the world.

BUILDING GENERATIONAL WEALTH

I read in a special book that a good man leaves an inheritance to his children's children. Women, we are not left out from this idea. We have to look out for our children and generations to come. I am so passionate about home-based businesses because a lot of times, they can be passed on to family members in the time of death; therefore, you don't have to worry about your hard work being in vain. Imagine building a multimillion-dollar empire just by partnering up in a home-based business, doing the work, believing, self-improving, and staying focused for five to seven years! Is it worth it? How long would it take you to earn millions of dollars from your job? Working a job by itself results in getting rich slowly yet working a job and a part-time business creates wealth. We can no longer depend on just a job to help our families, and your job alone is not building generational wealth; you are more or less building someone's else's dreams.

Remember what I said wealth is: income-producing assets that allow you to live the type of lifestyle you want to live regardless of going to work. Think about the things you can do one time and continue to get paid for the rest of your life. If you are clueless, start with a home-based business in network marketing, and you will get the training you need, grow your intellectual property, and build generational wealth! Don't worry, we can and will help you. Start working on your financial statement—and be honest about it—track your spending and become a Wealth Creator. You can become a Wealth Creator by joining our University. Go to **www.twcuniversity.com** to get training on taxes, finances, wealth creation, investing, marketing, real-estate, etc. Our university is available 24/7, with training modules to help you grow in the specific areas you need help in. Now, let's go out there and build wealth!

Chapter 6

DESIGNING YOUR FUTURE: THE SCIENCE TO BECOMING WEALTHY

THERE IS A lot to be said in this chapter, and I could easily turn this chapter into a book itself. However, I will do my absolute best to be so specific and to the point that even a five-year-old would understand this information. I would like to reference the Holy Bible in stating this chapter—to be exact, Habakkuk 2:2: "And the Lord answered me, and said, write the vision, and make it plain upon the tables, that he may run that readeth it."

Look at the instruction in that verse: you must first write the vision.

Whose vision? Your Vision. Think about your personal goals.

Then make the vision plain, so when you write it and read it, you will go to work.

WRITE THE VISION

Have you ever heard the saying "Out of sight, out of mind"? This simply means if you don't see it, you will not pay attention to it, and it will just become one of those things, another goal. Write your vision. What are your dreams or goals? Do you have specific goals that you would love to accomplish?

Start with writing down ten goals that you would like to achieve this year, then I want you to circle the number-one goal that you must achieve. This goal has to be a burning desire—I mean, you have to be thinking, *Out of all the goals I have written, this is the do-or-die goal.*

Next, I want you to write that goal at the top of another piece of paper, then write a question. For example, if your goal is to earn $100,000 this year, write the question, "What must I do this year to earn $100,000 dollars?"

Now, begin to brainstorm. Take a few minutes to ponder the question, focusing only on that question. As the answers begin to fill your head, start writing them down on paper. See if you can come up with twenty answers—twenty is the magic number. Once you have the answers, I want you to start applying your answers to your life every day. Work on your goal each day and stay focused! Distractions will come, disappointments will come, doubt and fear will come; however, stay focused.

F.O.C.U.S. = Follow One Course Until Successful!

Remember to be patient. You will get frustrated sometimes but kill that negative emotion! I want you to be happy and grateful that your goal is going to happen.

Verse 3 of Habakkuk 2 states, "For the vision is yet for an appointed time, but at the end it shall speak, and not lie."

So many people fail and give up because they don't see their goals happening fast enough; they are not patient and truly don't believe that reaching their goals will ever happen. These people allow outside influences, whispers, and voices in their head to tell them their goals are not going to happen. I remember telling this lady I was going to be a multimillionaire, and she laughed and said, "Girl, stop chasing a pipe dream." Now, if I had low self-esteem, this lady probably would have gotten the best of me, but I believe in a source bigger than myself. Greater is He that is in the world! I believe in God; He is my source. I am not religious; however, I am spiritual, and my belief is when you are working on something you have never done before, you must rely on a "higher power" than yourself.

USE ALL OF YOUR STRENGTH

God has given you the power to create. Call on Him, and He will give you want you need, place people in your path to help you, and bring ideas into your head to expand your vision. Then the "magic" begins to happen! Remember, all things are possible to them who believe. Believe bigger, believe for more...

When it comes to having a dream or goal, here are some facts to help you and to ensure that you never quit:

Henry Ford went broke five times before he succeeded.

Quaker Oats, Pepsi Cola, Birds Eye Frozen Food, and Wrigley's Gum all filed for bankruptcy three times before they were successful.

The key to success is to refuse to quit, to refuse to give up! No matter what it looks like, no matter what people think about you, continue to keep going, for your victory is with God. He made you victorious! You are more than a conqueror; you are successful, and I want you to know that I believe in you and love you!

MAKE IT PLAIN

At one seminar, I was teaching about the tax advantages of owning a home-based business, and I asked a specific question. I asked, "What is financial freedom to you?" Most people said, "The freedom to go anywhere I want, with whoever I want." One lady said, "Being able to buy what I want and not having to worry about money." Lastly, a gentleman stated, "Time freedom and money freedom." I smiled and stated that they were all wrong, and they looked at me quite strangely. I told them that everything they mentioned was the result of what money could do for them, but "financial freedom" is a quantitative figure.

Earlier, I mentioned that you have to know what that specific amount is and then you can begin to work on your plan to achieve it. Make it plain; be specific with your goal setting. Don't be vague because this will not allow you to achieve your goals. If you want to get rid of weight, state how many pounds you want to lose. If you want to earn a six-figure yearly income, specify the amount, and put a date by it! If you want to get married, write down what you are looking for and be specific; include the date you want to get married. Please make sure that what you are asking for, you are that yourself! Be fair in the asking; water seeks it owns level, so you might need to change yourself (that is another subject)!

For the most part, most people don't even know what they want, and they are definitely not specific about their goals. "Without goals, and plans to reach them, you are like a ship that has set sail with no destination."

In conclusion with making your goal plain, make sure your goal is specific. Have an action plan, set a reasonable date, manage your expectations, and discipline your disappointments. It will happen. Review your plan daily and seek a mentor for help—and make sure you are getting advice from qualified sources!

All you need is a little LUC. Our coaching/mentoring company, Level Up Coaching, is here to help you take your business, your dreams, and your life to another level. If you would like a free fifteen-minute consultation, you can go to our website **www.thelucfirmllc.com** for all the details. No more excuses. Help is on the way if you are interested.

READ IT AND RUN WITH IT!

Now that you have written your goal and have made it very plain, it is time to execute your plan! You need to make sure that once you have written your action plan, you review your goals daily. Go get some 3x5-inch index cards and write your goals on those cards as though they have already happened. For example, you could write:

- "I am so happy and grateful now that I earn over $100,000 dollars a month from my wealth creation company."
- "I am so happy and grateful now that I am healthy and at my perfect weight of 135 lbs. and I am a size 9/10."

These are only examples, so write your goals accordingly. When you add gratitude to your goal, I bear witness that it speeds up the process of achieving that goal. Pick five goals and write them as I stated: "I am so happy and grateful now that..."

Read your goals every day, and always be excited when you read them. Have the deep-seated belief that your goal is already accomplished. After you read your goals, run, don't walk, and immediately get into action mode. Take the right action steps that your mentor has given you. If you don't have a mentor, contact our office, and we would be honored to help you at Wealthy Women Enterprises or TIFFIS, LLC.

The purpose of the cards is so you can carry them wherever you go and read them on a daily basis, then your subconscious mind can begin to help you meet who you need in order to bring your goals into fruition. You must have the faith as well as the work effort. Just sitting around reading your goals and not working toward them is what we call "imaginary craziness." Faith without works is dead, so go to work!

Everything I just mentioned will help you design your future. Thoughts become things.

In the beginning of creation was the Word of God therefore, you have to begin with the word. Every millionaire with whom I have spoken began with a thought that became a goal that went into action and eventually became a reality. The science to becoming wealthy is knowing what you want and only focusing on what you want, then designing the plan, believing in it, and getting to work. Only share your goals with those you know believe in you! Not everyone is happy for you, and you must know this. Surround yourself with like-minded people, people who add value to your life and whose lives you add value to as well.

In the personal development chapter, I mentioned to read every day, study those who are successful, and emulate them. Find someone who is successful and take on their habits. You will have to sacrifice some things—I am being honest! To get what you want, you have to have a burning desire for it. You have to become your own biggest fan. No matter what it looks like, keep believing, keep working, and refuse to give up. The genius to becoming wealthy or successful is not just learning wealth principles, discovering the secret to success, or ever finding the right cat to copy. The real secret to success is…

You ready for this? You sure? Can you handle it?

NEVER, EVER QUIT!

Chapter 7

HOW TO ACHIEVE TOTAL PROSPERITY IN EVERY AREA OF YOUR LIFE

ERRIAM-WEBSTER DEFINES PROSPERITY as: the condition of being successful or thriving good fortune. 2. Economic well-being

I love the words "thriving," "successful," and "flourishing." When I talk about "total prosperity" in every area of your life, I like to say that you are thriving and successful mentally, physically, financially, spiritually, emotionally, as well as relationally. You are flourishing in all of these areas, and you have the total prosperity pie!

If you have all the money in the world yet you have poor health, I guarantee you that you would focus only on your health and not your money. If you are healthy but are living in poor conditions, you would be constantly thinking about your lack of money. I want you to flourish in each of the six areas I mentioned above. Ask yourself, "How do I achieve total prosperity in every area of my life?"

Many people have wondered if two driven individuals, both of whom are very successful and have happy marriages, could be jealous of each other? Can you be spiritually connected to God while being extraordinarily rich? Can you be successful and still have peace of mind?

The answer, my friend, is yes. I will cover each of these six areas separately to help you understand how to achieve total prosperity and flourish in every area of your life!

MENTALLY: "HAVING PEACE OF MIND & THE RIGHT MINDSET"

I want to start off with some definitions to let you know where I am going with this section.

Peace: freedom from disturbance; quietness and tranquility.

Mindset: an attitude, a disposition, or a mood; an intention or inclination; the ideas and attitudes with which a person approaches a situation, especially when these are seen as being difficult to alter.

How do you have peace of mind? Remember, I am sharing my beliefs with you and what works for me. You can use my suggestions, read others, then apply what you feel will work for you. In Philippians 4:6-7, I read that you are "to be careful for nothing (worry about nothing) but in everything by prayer and supplication with thanksgiving let your requests be made known unto God...and the peace of God, which passes all understanding shall keep your hearts and minds through Christ Jesus."

I understand that this verse means that we should cast our worries, doubts, fears, and concerns upon God, then give Him the praise (celebrate Him) for answering our prayers. Then He will give us His peace that passes all understanding.

I have peace of mind because I pray and believe God answers all of my prayers. I believe that once I pray, what I have asked for is done. Once I pray, I don't worry. Sometimes doubt will begin to creep up, and that's when I begin to praise God for the answers to my problems; then the doubt goes away.

I believe that the source of all my power is God within. When I recognize I can do all things through Him, I can face my fears. I have peace and understanding. I don't allow negative people to be around me, and if I can help it, I don't even allow them in my life. Misery loves company, and it can also disturb your peace. Stay away from negative disturbances, gossip, slack talk, jealousy, and envy because all of these things will rob you of your peace of mind. Just remember that you can't worry and pray at the same time. Pray and celebrate, and you will have peace of mind.

I have peace when I know I am being true to myself and doing what makes me happy. One thing I discovered I love to do is write in my journal. I also love to sing, dance, laugh, and I play, and I enjoy being around true friends and family.

Here's another suggestion: stop trying to please everyone! Let the church say, "Amen." Listen, it will not happen. Early in life, I learned that I can't make everyone happy, for that is impossible. Even trying to do this will definitely kill your peace of mind. I heard that only a fool tries to please everyone, so stop trying. You deserve peace, and you can have it when you rely on the source of all your power, God within!

MINDSET

I believe having a positive mental attitude will also give you prosperity mentally. One day, I was listening to a speaker at a seminar, and he stated that when we have problems in our lives, we need to remember that only 10 percent of our issue is the problem, while the other 90 percent is how we solve the problem.

How is your attitude? Do people like you? Are you extremely negative? Do you look for the bad in every situation? Are you a problem causer or a problem solver? The answers to all these questions have something to do with your mindset. A great mindset starts with being positive, being a problem solver, as well as how you approach issues on a daily basis.

I could go really deep into mindset, but I promise to explain this more in another book. However, I encourage you to be honest with yourself, answer the questions I just asked you, and then begin to work on how you see things. Every day, accentuate the positive and look for solutions. Work on your personal development by reading books, attending self-help seminars, getting counseling, and praying each day.

I am aware that some of our beliefs have been placed within us through our parents and our upbringing, yet even though we are born looking like our parents, we die looking like our decision. Therefore, I believe in talking to counselors and coaches to help you develop the right mental attitude. If you desire to have a positive mindset, then you should begin by working on yourself. You become what you think about most of the time, so you can begin to change your thoughts and work on finding peace of mind and a healthy mindset!

SPIRITUALLY

I stated earlier that you have to believe in a source that is higher than yourself. I believe in God and infinite wisdom. I genuinely believe that prayer answers things, and I have experienced the power of prayer. When I talk about spirituality, I mainly like to focus on becoming one with the Creator, tapping into the source of His power, and bringing out the gifts He has placed in us. I know there is power in the Word of God, so I believe in studying the Word, gaining understanding, and applying God's principles in my life.

I believe to truly know God is to know thyself. My spiritual belief is to serve God, obey God, be a shepherd to His sheep, be good to my fellow man, and multiply the talents my Creator has given me. I believe that belief in the unknown, the power of the living Word, or the spiritual vibration in oneself, as well as mastering who you are, are all true examples of being spiritual, in my eye. I want for my brother and sister what I want for myself! I want to please God, and I please God by tapping into His infinite wisdom to serve His purpose, and then I become a Master of my Universe.

Spirituality is being one with the Creator, one with self, and mastering the mind He gave you. To serve others, to love freely, to understand, to seek forgiveness, and to forgive are all traits of God. To submit your will to the will of God, to surrender to Him, and to believe in Him for guidance and understanding will help you on your spiritual walk.

I remember hearing someone I truly admire, Ms. Oprah Winfrey, a billionaire, talk about her experience with wanting to be in the movie *The Color Purple*. She stated that she read the book several times, gave the book away to several people, and could see herself in the character she read. She wanted to be in the movie so badly that she was blessed with a script, but she was told it wasn't *The Color Purple*; still, she was asked to read for them. She read the script and knew the characters by heart; she knew this was exactly what she had been asking for. After reading, she was told she would be contacted if the interest was there. Time went on, and she heard nothing. She waited with anticipation…still no answer. She began to doubt herself. She said that she had thought about her weight, thinking maybe that was why she hadn't received the role, so she decided to go to what she called "a fat farm" to lose weight.

Now, jumping ahead of what she shared, Oprah said she was walking on the track one day, feeling overwhelmed and almost giving up, so she decided to surrender her will and started singing, "I surrender all, all to Thee my precious Savior, I surrender all!" The point I like to make is she surrendered. She gave it to God, and guess what, she was blessed with the part she wanted. Oprah tapped into the source and submitted to God. I genuinely believe she became one with Him in song and praise and her prayer was answered.

You have to find what your spiritual walk is and what you believe. Tap into the source by prayer, reading the Word, confessing what you believe every day, and staying firm in your belief.

When my coach and friend, multimillionaire Edward Hartley, was training, he would always say to us, "Surrender your will and secure your wealth." Wealth is more than money, and I hope you are gaining this understanding now as I break down these six parts of total prosperity. I believe when you surrender your will, this allows spiritual forces to intervene and place you where you need to be!

PHYSICALLY

The mind, the body, the soul. I have always been told that these three things will give you total peace if you manage them correctly. We talked about the mind, and we talked about the soul (spirituality). Now, let's explore the physical aspect of the prosperity pie, that being the body.

Throughout my journey in life, I have noticed that I gave my complete service to my children, often taking care of their needs before mine. I served my husband at that time, striving to be a good wife, but I never focused on my own physical needs. My children's father abandoned me, as you read in the beginning of this book, and I went through a slight depression after that. I gained weight and became someone other than myself. I thank God that I didn't have health challenges; however, I knew I had to get myself back to excellent physical health! Therefore, I started working out, loving myself more, paying attention to what I ate, fasting and praying, and taking pride in the way I looked. I made a promise to myself that I would never let myself go again.

I love myself, and I tell myself this every day. I get all my yearly checkups, exercise, eat the right foods, get massages, meditate, and really stay tuned in to my body. I sometimes take breaks and just go to a private spot, a vacation with just myself, to relieve stress; to meditate; to explore my mind; and of course, to release excess negative energy or thoughts from my mind, body, and soul.

I believe you must focus on personal healing, love yourself, and take really good care of your temple, your body. I am not completely where I want to be, but I tell you, personal physical health is a constant work in progress. I will never, ever be where I want to be, because I believe in constantly improving oneself.

You must look at yourself. Do you like what your physical body looks like? Are you healthy and in shape? How is your energy level? Are you angry and bitter? Depressed? Can't sleep? Overeating? Not happy? If you answered yes to any of these questions, you should most definitely seek a doctor's care to get the help you need.

Also, my recommendation would be to decide what you want. How do you want to look, feel, and be? Now, write it down. Begin to tap into your inner self. Be honest with yourself. Go on a fast and drink plenty of water. Water is life; it is the source of all living things, so you, my friend, need water. Drink life, take baby steps, and exercise, even if it's a thirty-minute walk every day. Do it! You will begin to feel more energized and excited about being you. The funny thing is when you get in front of the mirror and see the results, oh man, you will want to do a higher-impact workout because you will like what you see!

Listen, there is only one you, only one! Please love yourself; don't think someone is going to love you if you can't love yourself. We are visual people; we love to see people in great shape. Get healthy and get moving. You heard it before: "Move more, eat less." You must take care of your physical being, your temple. Do you want to live a long life? If you do, then act like it and start taking care of yourself.

Physical health is an everyday thing. It's a journey, so enjoy it. I promise you will love the results and love yourself more! The world is watching, so get yourself into excellent health. Take care of you! We want you around, so let's get moving. Bring sexy back! I love you, but you must love yourself!

Are you ready?

Let's get moving!

FINANCIALLY

I am laughing right now because I kind of cheated…I gave you a lot of knowledge about finances at the beginning of this book. Repetition is the mother of all learning; however, I want you to go back to the beginning of the book and read what I already talked to you about regarding getting your money right.

At this time, I would like you to go back and read Chapter 5, Increasing Your Financial IQ, What's Your Grade? Read it, answer the questions honestly, and begin putting together a plan to get you on the road to financial freedom.

Remember, you can't do it by yourself, so seek counseling. You can go to our website **www.tiffisllc.com** for assistance with taxes, finances, or wealth creation, or seek help from someone you know and trust who can help you achieve financial freedom. Focus on the end in mind, where you see yourself in the future. As I stated earlier, a job by itself just won't do, not now, not ever. Get your money right and create generational wealth. You deserve it!

EMOTIONALLY

If you use them properly, emotions can be beautiful. To show love, care, excitement, joy, and happiness are signs of being in alignment with our dreams and goals. However, emotions can also be dangerous; they can destroy the very thing we worked so hard to achieve. To show anger, fear, jealously, doubt, and sadness can take us away from our goal.

In the movie *"The Secret"* they reference the Emotional Guidance System. Your Emotional Guidance System is a simple guide that allows you to know if you are on track with your dreams and goals. An example would be if I am working in the spirit of gratitude, and I am thankful and excited about my future, then I am aligned with what I am asking for. When I am angry, jealous, doubtful, or feeling depressed and unappreciated, these emotions allow me to realize that I am out of alignment of what I want; therefore, I need to pray and fast as well as reflect on why I am feeling this way. I need to change my frequency so I can get back into my happy zone.

As women, we are very emotional beings. I tell you! I love being a woman, but good grief, we can be over the top! When you move out on the wrong emotional vibration, it can be destructive to your universe. I used to get so upset when I would hear men say that women are emotional. Later, however, I learned that we are the nurturers, the teachers, and the caretakers, so we therefore have strong emotions, as they are part of our nature.

I embrace my womanhood, but I have learned and am still learning how to monitor my emotions. If I am too excited or terribly angry, I sit down, reflect, and bring myself to a happy medium point so I can focus clearly. If you are too emotional and move too quickly, remember that the result may not be what you intend it to be. Pay attention to your Emotional Guidance System. Make sure your emotions are not too high or too low. Listen to yourself and your spirit of discernment, and the end result will be a positive note.

Women, we have been given these emotions for a reason. We are Mothers, Friends, Wives, Lovers, Businesswomen, Sisters, etc. Our love, our care, and even our emotions are all needed. I am just expressing that you must monitor your emotions, keep them in check, get counseling for past pain if you need it, and let the healing begin. You were given your emotions as a guide, so allow them to be thus so.

Be happy and feel good! Remember, too much of anything is not good, so keep high vibrations, feel good, and rejoice in your blessings to come.

RELATIONALLY

Wow, we talked about prospering mentally, spiritually, physically, financially, and emotionally, which now brings us to the last part of the prosperity pie: building strong relationships.

We are products of our environment. What we read, what we listen to, what we watch, and the people we hang around shape us. Please, I implore you to be careful about who you hang around, as those in your life can make you or break you! Several times a day, I say this affirmation: "I only surround myself around people who add value to me, and in return, I add value to them."

I look for valuable relationships. People who I can learn from, who inspire me, who encourage me, who hold me accountable, and who believe in me. In short, I go where I am celebrated, not where I am tolerated!!!

My mother always said, "Birds of a feather flock together." If you want to truly know who you are, examine your relationships and friendships. Thought's travel, and a lot of times, we are moving not on our own accord but on the thoughts of others. We need people in our lives but be careful who you choose to give your valuable time to.

I can't tell you who to build relationships with, but I can say that in my life, I have noticed that we sometimes build addictive relationships that are harmful to us and tear at every fiber of our being. I want you to do this exercise right now: Write down the names of your closest friends, then list the pros and cons about each of them. Then ask yourself, "Are these people adding value to me or taking away my value?" Please answer this question honestly. Maybe you are not ready for total prosperity in every area of your life. There has to be a season of separation from the things or people that are hindering you from your true growth potential.

I am a Deliberate Creator. I only surround myself with those who add value to my life and whose lives I add value to. Relationships are powerful. Be aware of who you are around; don't be like a cork in the water, wandering and drifting on with no directions. Know who you are and whose you are and seek out the right people who can guide you along the way.

I was talking to a dear friend of mine about relationships, and we discovered that people come into your life for four reasons: for a season, for a reason, for a lifetime, or for a lesson. You must understand this and know that people come, and people go, and where you are going in your life, not everyone will be able to go with you. This was the hardest reality I had to face. As painful as it was, I had to grasp this understanding that not everyone is going where God wants me to go, and I had to come to grips with the fact that this is ok. Greater is on the other side. You will meet new people to help you get to your destination. That's great; embrace that fact. Don't be afraid to let go of excess baggage. You deserve to be in the best relationships possible. Whether friendships, a marriage, partnerships, or personal relationships, make sure the people in your life are truly who you need to grow and go to the top! If not, drop them like a hot potato.

Stop being fake and hanging around people you can't stand to be around only because of name recognition or status. Be true to you. What do you want? Can this person help you with your process? If not, move on! I pride myself on building powerful relationships. I am excited to meet the new friends, business partners, and mastermind alliances.

It's not who you know; rather, I like to say that "who knows you" is what makes a big difference in your world. Be true and build powerful, loving, wealthy, and healthy relationships!

Chapter 8

TO THINE OWN SELF BE TRUE: THE POWER OF SELF-DISCOVERY

HMMM. "TO THINE own self be true." I know you have heard of this phrase or quote before but let me share with you my thoughts about being true to oneself.

The greatest discovery in this life that you will experience or should be chasing is the discovery of oneself. We often beat ourselves up and go into depression because we feel we should be light years ahead of where we currently are. We don't realize that life is a process, a journey into becoming who you will be.

Something else that we do that is very damaging is compare ourselves to others. At different times in my life, I know I have been guilty of observing others that I consider successful and comparing their journey to my journey. This is definitely a way of self-sabotaging your whole outlook in life and missing out on learning what is necessary to take you to the next level.

I heard someone say, "Do not compete but create; this is where happiness lies."

AM I GOOD ENOUGH?

Earlier, I told you about how I went on a 100-city tour with very popular celebrities and millionaires. I remember the day before our first seminar, I was looking at the lineup for the event in my mind, and fear began to creep in. Everyone who was speaking on the tour was already a documented millionaire, and at the time, I wasn't! I started to feel unqualified, unworthy to be on the stage with the "big boys." However, I quickly realized that I was already a millionaire because success starts in the mind first!

We first build or create in the mind, then on paper, and finally in the physical. I was qualified with my position as a former IRS auditor and a tax/financial expert at that time. I knew my subject matter and had countless testimonies from clients who utilize our services, but there went that comparison. I began looking outward at the millions the other speakers had versus the millions I had not yet acquired for myself. You see why comparing yourself to others is not good and is really damaging? I would have quit the conference if I had allowed myself to focus on what I didn't have versus what I do have, knowing that I am enough!

Later, I gained the understanding that every experience, every lesson, every trial, every victory was leading me to the woman I was becoming and the woman I am now. I am more than enough, and I have the power to achieve whatever my mind can conceive!

I want you to say that to yourself right now. "I am enough." Repeat it! "I am enough." Now, believe it! Don't doubt yourself. Everything you are going through, growing through, and learning through is carrying you to the bigger vision and dream ahead. Don't compare, just create, and watch the world you find yourself in. It is utterly amazing when you realize and declare, "I am good enough!"

WHAT ARE "THEY" SAYING ABOUT ME?

How many times have you ever thought to yourself or admitted that you were concerned about what others, or "they," were thinking about you or saying about you?

When I decided to let go of one phase of my business and re-brand myself and create other divisions of our company, I began to hear those whispers of doubt in my mind. "What makes you qualified to coach or mentor?" "How much money have you made?" "What are people going to say?" "Who does she think she is?"

I finally had to scream out loud, "ENOUGH!"

It is none of my darn business what people think or say about me. My business is what I think and say about myself! For me, freedom was letting go of the negative thoughts and opinions of others as well as the doubts that creep in and only allow myself to focus on the positive.

It is truly a blessing to not focus on the big question: "What do they think?" You have to practice this because this question will always try to pop up and make you weak and vulnerable. But when you can let go and let God, and focus on being 100 percent yourself, you will find total freedom!

I am totally loving myself all over again. I am discovering new things about myself all the time, and I am learning why I went through some of the difficult things in my life—so I could be a beacon of light to others. Now, my lessons are somebody else's blessings, and my pain is a gift to help others achieve their dreams. My joys are proof that every test you experience can and will be part of your testimony. I already discussed that my purpose in life is to be a great impact on a billion lives, and it's none of my business how that will be done. All I need to do is go out there and live big, love long, go hard, and go strong. Life is for the living, and I choose to live life fully. All praises belong to God!

IT'S NOT ALL ABOUT ME

Oh, how many of us have asked the question "Why me, oh Lord?" Well, I will be the first to raise my hand. Long ago, I thought that God was mad at me. I never thought I would be abandoned, homeless, hungry, lonely, afraid, angry, doubtful, and hopeless.

I never would have believed that I would be abandoned with four beautiful lives to take care of, to teach, and to nurture past my own pain. There were days when I didn't know where my next meal was coming from. I was stretching the dollar bills to take care of my children.

The best gift my mom gave me was teaching me the power of prayer. Although she passed on to her next assignment on December 26, 2017, she is ever present, and I hear her voice louder now than I did when she was physically here. My mom, Minnie Gamble, was a praying soul, and she taught me to trust in God, to believe and know that all things work together for the good!

In the past, I didn't know that I was chosen to go into the world and help those who felt the same way I did when I felt alone, abandoned, afraid, doubtful, fearful, and unable to trust or believe. See, I now believe and know that "my life" is not all about me. My story is changing every day. God is fair and just, and He is always listening to us and answering prayer. I want you to know that God is listening to you. Your prayers are being answered too!

By reading this book, I know you will be impacted to make a change and walk into your full potential. Somebody is waiting for you to get out of the pain you are in and walk into your greatness. It's not all about me, and it's not all about you. Everything that you have been through and are now going through will propel you to greatness, if only you believe and receive this.

Your purpose is way bigger than you could imagine. Your story is not over. It's time to believe and dream again.

Let your story be your glory. Let your pain be your gain.

Somebody is waiting for your breakdown and your build up to be their breakthrough. When times are more challenging than others, remember this: "this too shall pass!" It's not all about me. I have the victory! It is done!

NEW CHAPTERS

One of the most difficult times in life can be when you realize that change is definite. As people, we do not really care for change. We get amazingly comfortable and used to how things are or how they used to be. I am told that your comfort zone is your broke zone. When you get too comfortable, you do not allow growth or new ideas to be introduced in your life. Now, I see why challenges are necessary to bring about "change," or as I like to call it, "new chapters."

Let me give you a couple of examples:

I have multiple streams of income because my mentors taught me to have that for security, yet a few years ago, one of my streams of income, a business I was working in, was running dry. I knew I needed to let it go, but because of the relationships I had with some of my team and other members, I was having a hard time leaving it. One day, one of my mentors called me to express that he was leaving the business and gave me his reasons. Because of whom this person was and the level he was at, I knew this was validation for me to let go, let God, and trust God.

See, I was nervous about the change. I had to learn to listen more to myself and not worry about what others would think or say. It was very funny to me that one of the people I was concerned about was leaving as well. I am so grateful for that phone call because it allowed me to enter an uncomfortable position and, more importantly, a position of self-discovery and truth.

By beginning a new chapter, I was able to rebrand myself, create my own products and services, and guess what? With my new brand, I made six figures in four months, then turned around and made six figures again in less than three months. I have gone on to create several streams of income, and money is not an issue.

Imagine staying in something that is dead and does not grow. If you do not leave, you too will begin to die inside and outside. Pay attention to the signs, trust your gut, and don't be afraid to end one chapter and start a new one.

HAVING 20/20 CLEAR & PERFECT VISION

I think I knew all along that if I could focus long enough, work long enough, and discover long enough, I would pinpoint my purpose, my dream, and my vision. Only when we take our eyes off of our goals and look at others can we get distracted and allow our vision to become blurred. If you are not prepared, looking at the success of other people can easily take you off of the path you need to be on and put you in a place of competition and fear. You will begin to feel that you will never catch up to someone else's success and that somehow you will reach your desired dream and goals. Now, instead of walking in abundance, you are living in scarcity, competition, fear, and jealousy.

But There Is Hope!

Live in the place of Creation. When I decided to not care about what "they" think or say about me, I began to have clear and perfect vision. Now, my focus is only on what God thinks about me. Am I fulfilling the dreams and the abilities that my Creator placed within me? For me, prayer and fasting became a door to help me clearly see what my purpose is! They helped me open a door to possibilities, abundance, greatness, and humility. I was then able to see beauty, intelligence, and creativity all around me. I felt like something had been unlocked in me and that God was smiling down on me because I discovered Me!

I knew that discipline, planning, and activity would give birth to all my dreams and would keep my vision clear from distraction, which is a known enemy.

One evening, I was on a webinar doing some much-needed personal development when I heard a young lady state, "There are five things' multimillionaires do before 8:00 a.m. every day." She being to list those five things, so I wrote them down. I studied those five things and then I decided to tweak the list and make it mine. I promised to myself that I would do these things every day until I reached a place of "unconscious competent," which simply means that you have mastered an activity and can do it without thought. For example, once you have mastered driving a car, you no longer drive with your hands at ten and two. You can eat and play music while you drive and even drive with one hand.

What are my five things? Thanks for asking. Here you go.

1) Prayer and Meditation

I start each day with thanks and appreciation for all that has been done, will be done, and continues to be done for me and my family.

2) Stretch/Exercise

Conditioning of the body is especially important. I am getting stronger every day. I work out each day, even when I don't feel like it, because it creates the discipline I need, which follows me throughout the day.

3) Review My Goals Daily

I must make sure I know what my purpose is and what I am attracting. I confirm in the spiritual and the physical that what I am attracting is already done!

4) Personal Development

Every morning, I take time to study books, videos, and training that allow me to continue to work on myself and become a better me each day. I believe in feeding my mind, body, and soul.

5) Execution of the Day (Agenda)

I look at my calendar for the agenda of the day and make sure that I execute all of the day's goals to the best of my ability. No excuses, no laziness— just straight execution. I allow myself to fail my way to success, to learn what is needed, to throw away that which is not, and to be willing to make adjustments happily.

These five things keep me on point and help me to have the clear and perfect vision I need to make my dreams reality. You can do this too! What will be the five things you do every day before 8:00 a.m.?

WILL IT EVER END?

I am always growing, changing, learning, adjusting, becoming. I don't think we ever reach a place in life where we say, "I have arrived! I am done." The minute we say that, we begin to die. It is said that less than two years after people retire, they are out of here dead. Why?

I believe we are on a continuous journey. Success is always changing, and once you finally reach it, it changes again! Therefore, it never ends; we are to stay progressive in a state of always becoming, always growing, always learning, always sharing.

The only time it ends is when you die. So, get busy living, or get busy dying.

YOU HAVE PERMISSION TO SUCCEED!

I believe you were born on this planet to do great things. You don't need anyone's permission, blessings, validation, or approval to do what God put into you to do! See, I don't think there is only one thing for us to do. I believe there are a myriad of things in us which are brought out through trials, conditions, and pain. Pain is a gift that no one wants to receive, yet it gives birth to new conditions, new decisions, and new opportunities for growth.

I believe our environment helps to shape the decisions we make, which enables us to determine the steps we take. In turn, this equips us to walk fully into our destination.

You already have all the power you need to be successful. You already have permission to succeed. Every day, we are learning more about ourselves. The people, places, and encounters we come across are all a part of our self-discovery.

I now understand what Romans 8:28 means when it says, "And we know that all things work together for good to them that love God, to them who are called according to his purpose." Everything, I mean everything—the good, the bad, and the ugly—is working toward your purpose. I believe that more now than I ever have, and trust me, I been through some ish! I used to think that God had left me, but He hadn't. He was preparing me for greatness.

I hope you know this for yourself. You are greatly made—perfectly made. Therefore, be true to yourself. Make no excuses as you continue to discover you! You have a story that others want to hear, and many will walk into their greatness because of you! I hope you know that nothing worth having comes easily. However, I believe your future will be greater than your past! Here's to discovering yourself, being true to yourself, and enjoying the journey.

It's only just begun!

CONCLUSION

WHEN I BEGAN working on this book in 2009, as I stated earlier, I had just come off a speaking tour with my good friend and father figure Danny Glover, my good friend Ken Rolfsness, and my wonderful friend Jack Zufelt. I was excited and started working on this book, my baby. I had to come to a halt when some obstacles came in my life, but no worries. It was indeed a struggle and a labor of love, but I meet and overcome all of the obstacles in my path.

At the end of 2013, I then began working on my project again. I went through personal development and personal healing. I had to forgive and forget. I had to embrace my talents, skills, and abilities. Most of all, I had to love myself in every way possible.

Now, we have come to the conclusion of this powerful book. My deepest, most sincere goal was and is that my words impact you in such a way that you too decide to be a Wealthy Woman because you refuse to be abused! It's your time! You deserve total happiness, joy, peace, love, wealth, health, and abundance.

I covered a lot in this book. I told you what made me decide to walk in the abundance of God's glory and be the best I can be in every area of my life. The old me had to die in order to give birth to the new me. I was truthful and honest with you, as well as transparent. All I ask you to do is be the same to yourself. Remember, the truth shall set you free!

Guys, I did a lot of personal development in my life. I prayed, I fasted, I cried, I laughed, I forgave myself, and I kept it moving. I believed that I should have total prosperity in every area of my life, so each day, I worked on every area the best I could. I have to say, guys, I am getting in shape every day.

I am the first millionaire—and not the last—in my family. I have peace of mind and a oneness with the Creator, and I seek guidance from God in all things. I am emotionally whole, and guess what? On May 30, 2015, God blessed me with my soulmate, a man who not only supports me but shows me that he loves me the way I deserve to be loved, each and every day. He is my best friend, my companion, my business partner, my lover...a gift from God. I want you to believe that you deserve total happiness, and I encourage you to start claiming it right now! I also know now why

God blessed me with this man at this time because together we will fulfill the purpose he placed in our lives. He is the rock that I stand on and it is a blessing to have a good friend, provider, lover, and husband.

I pray you read this book and say, "You know what, If Jean did it, I can do it too." A good friend of mine said, "Pain is a gift that no one wants to receive." Mr. Athon Clemons taught me that. I thank him for sharing this with me.

His point is correct. Out of my pain, trials, and suffering, this book will touch millions of lives! Read this book over and over again, buy five or more copies, give them to your friends, and even do these exercises together. We want you to keep in contact with us and let us know how we helped to impact your life.

Be on the lookout for many more books to come. We will give you all these details at the end of the book. Remember, in life, it does no good to have one or two slices of the prosperity pie; you must have total prosperity in every area of your life.

Now, I have a special treat for you, it is especially important that you have an accountability partner in your life to help you stay true to your word. What better accountability partner to have than Jean Marlo Davis? I want you to take the Wealthy Woman Pledge with me! I want you to say it every morning after prayer and right before you go to bed. I encourage you to make sure you are a woman of your word!

Take the pledge, believe in yourself, love yourself, and let your conscience be your guide!

I want to hear how your life has changed and what you have done to make a difference, not just in your life but in the lives of others. You are beautiful, you are smart, you are sexy, you are healthy, and you are wealthy!

You are a Wealthy Woman because you refuse to be abused!

I love you!

Hugs and kisses…

Now, take the pledge on the next page! God bless you, wealthy woman!

WEALTHY WOMAN PLEDGE

WEALTHY WOMAN PLEDGE:

I, (your name), hereby authorize, command, demand, and acknowledge that I am a Wealthy Woman because I refuse to be abused.

I am a Wealthy Woman because I am out of debt, my needs are met, and I have plenty more to put in store.

I am a Wealthy Woman because money comes to me easily, effortlessly, and continually in ever-increasing amounts.

I am a Wealthy Woman because I am blessed to be a blessing.

I am a Wealthy Woman because I also seek knowledge to expand my growth and development, as well as the kingdom of God.

I am a Wealthy Woman because I take care of my temple, my body. I feed my body healthy food, I exercise daily, and I maintain a healthy weight. I also feed my mind with positive, inspiring, and healthy thoughts that will continue to force me to grow to be the Woman of God I should be.

I declare I am a Wealthy Woman because I am the righteousness of God. I continue to seek God's face for my spiritual growth, complete directions, and my assignment He has given unto me to glorify His good works. To God is the glory forever!

I promise that I will not allow myself to be abused in any manner, by anyone, including but not limited to myself. I will not be abused mentality, spiritually, physically, financially, or emotionally any longer, for I am a Wealthy Woman because I refuse to be abused!

I, (your name), accept this pledge, commit to this pledge, and will help other women become Wealthy Women this (date) day of (month), (present year).

Now, say this every day and mean it; make it happen. You are now a Wealthy Woman!

I love you!
Your Servant and Friend,
Jean Marlo Davis

*****BONUS*****

By purchasing this book, you are entitled to 10% off all TIFFIS, LLC, TWC, The LUC Firm & WWE products and services for 1 year. To claim your discount and be updated on upcoming events, workshops, webinars, etc., go to www.twcuniversity.com, fill out the form, and text us at 678-457-9493 when ready to redeem, for discount code.

*****EXTRA BONUS*****

My friends and many women around the world have asked me do we have a membership page, a support group, or something where they can continue to meet up and grow with one another?

Well ladies, at the launch of this book we created our WWE Support You membership page. You can go here and get support with losing weight and getting in shape with (Sexy 15 with Jean). Financial & Investing Support, Networking, Business Building, Coaching, Relationship and so much more. If you want to be a part of the first 1000 members go to www.wwesupportyou.com and register now and continue to grow, learn, educate, build, and unite as a Wealthy Woman Who Wins!!!

FOLLOW US ON SOCIAL MEDIA:

Youtube.com/jeanmarlodavis
Facebook.com/yourwealthcreator
Instagram.com/mrsjeanmarlodavis
Twitter.com/jeanmarlodavis

Thank you again, and congratulations!

WWE look forward to meeting all the exceptional women around the world who believes they too are a Wealthy Woman, and you refuse to be abused....

Your Wealth Creator,
Jean Marlo Davis XOXOXO

REFERENCE PAGE

Ellevest Team, (Article Online: What women Can do about Divorce Inequality) Published 11/8/2018

Laurie Itkin, Next Avenue Contributor (Forbes Article Online: The 6 Nasty Financial surprises for Divorcing Women) Published 7/15/18

Fitzhugh, Dodson (Quotes 4176#) quoteland.com **Without goals, and plans to reach them, you are like a ship that has set sail with no destination**.

Merriam-Webster (defines prosperity online) as: the condition of being successful or thriving good fortune. 2. Economic well-being

Clemons, Athon (Quote: "Pain is a gift that no one wants to receive.")

CPSIA information can be obtained
at www.ICGtesting.com
Printed in the USA
BVHW071407210921
617189BV00002B/74